A DOCUMENTARY HISTORY
OF THE HOLOCAUST™

# JEWISH RESISTANCE AGAINST THE HOLOCAUST

ROBERT Z. COHEN

ROSEN
PUBLISHING®

New York

Published in 2015 by The Rosen Publishing Group, Inc.
29 East 21st Street, New York, NY 10010

First Edition

**Library of Congress Cataloging-in-Publication Data**

Cohen, Robert Z.
Jewish resistance against the Holocaust/Robert Z. Cohen.—First edition.
    pages cm.—(A documentary history of the Holocaust)
Includes bibliographical references and index.
ISBN 978-1-4777-7601-8 (library bound)
1. World War, 1939-1945—Jewish resistance. 2. World War, 1939-1945—
Participation, Jewish. 3. Holocaust, Jewish (1939-1945) I. Title.
D810.J4C586 2015
940.53'1832—dc23

2013045597

*Manufactured in the United States of America*

# CONTENTS

# INTRODUCTION

Both as a poet and a fighter, Abba Kovner (1918–1987) embodied the spirit of Jewish resistance. His thirst for revenge against the Nazis continued even after the war ended.

The destruction of Europe's Jews by the Nazis and their allies between 1938 and 1945 was an event unlike any in history, and it is remembered today as the Holocaust. To attempt to destroy an entire group of people—not soldiers, but unarmed civilians, men, women, and children—is genocide. The Holocaust, however, was unique in the way that the Nazis were determined to rid the world of all Jews. The Nazis were willing to sacrifice important military and economic goals to achieve the destruction of the Jews.

When we speak about the Holocaust it is often asked, "Why didn't the Jews fight back? Why did they go to their deaths without resisting?" The truth is that many did resist. Israeli Holocaust historian Yehuda Bauer points out that what is surprising is not how little Jewish resistance there was, but rather how much. There were many forms of resistance. Resistance can be found in the will to live when the enemy wishes otherwise. Resistance against a stronger enemy is never limited to the barrel of a gun.

The decision to rise up and fight against the Nazis was made by young people crowded into ghetto basements, the barracks of concentration camps, or hiding in dugout shelters in the woods of Europe. As they watched their friends and families taken to be shot, starved, or gassed, they realized their choice was between an anonymous death at the hands of the enemy or a powerful statement of defiance in the face of evil.

Such a statement was delivered on New Year's Eve, 1941, in a basement in the ghetto of Vilna (today Vilnius, Lithuania), according to Michael Bart in his book *Until Our Last Breath*, which chronicles the Jewish Resistance. A group of young Jews met to greet the New Year. A young poet named Abba Kovner raised his voice to be heard in the cold basement and read from a speech he had prepared. "Destroy your illusions" cried Kovner, "Let us not go like sheep to the slaughter!"

Kovner's declaration was rooted in Jewish history. In 63 BCE the ancient Jewish homeland in Judea became a protectorate of the Roman Empire. When the Jews rose in revolt against Rome in 70 CE, the Romans burned the Jewish city of Jerusalem and destroyed the Second Temple that had been the center of Jewish ceremonial life. One band of Jewish rebels refused to surrender. Retreating to a fortress perched atop Mount Masada, they fought the Roman armies to a standstill. In 73 CE, cut off from supplies and with no hope for rescue, the Jewish defenders of Masada chose to commit mass suicide rather than become Roman slaves. According to the Jewish Virtual Library, rebel leader Elazar ben Yair told his followers: "We were the very first that revolted, and we are the last to fight against them; and I cannot but esteem it as a favor that God has granted us, that it is still in our power to die bravely, and in a state of freedom."

When faced with destruction, sometimes the unthinkable solution becomes the only possible choice: Let us not go like sheep to the slaughter!

# CHAPTER 1

# BACKGROUND TO TRAGEDY

Jews living around the world consider themselves to be a part of a diaspora, or community living outside of their lost homeland. After the Roman War and the destruction of the Holy Temple, many Jews left the land of Judea to settle elsewhere, but they continued to maintain their lives and identity as defined by Jewish law and religion.

## THE ROOTS OF EUROPEAN JEWISH LIFE

Over the centuries Jewish communities grew around the Mediterranean basin. During the Greek and Roman empires, Jews had already set up trade networks and formed new communities in Europe. Over time, these communities developed their own identities, local customs, and languages. Jews who settled in the Roman provinces of Spain became known as Sephardic Jews, who spoke a form of medieval Spanish written using the Hebrew alphabet called Ladino. Muslim Arabs conquered Spain in 711 CE leading to a period known as the Golden Age of

Spanish Jewry: Sephardic Jewish learning and culture reached great heights, particularly in science and medicine.

Jewish communities to the north in the Frankish and German lands gradually adopted forms of the German language, producing their own Jewish language called Yiddish (which simply means "Jewish"). They became known as Ashkenazi Jews. Schools grew in Jewish communities to teach children (mainly boys) to read and write in both the Hebrew of the holy books and the Aramaic language of the Talmud, the book of oral law and Jewish custom. Girls learned to read at home in Yiddish, which became known as *mame loshen*, or mother's language.

# MEDEIVAL ANTISEMITISM

Jewish communities were at a disadvantage in medieval Europe. Labeled as Christ-killers, Jews were often attacked and run out of their settlements. Jews were often restricted to live only in certain neighborhoods of cities by law. These eventually became known as ghettos, after the name of the original walled-in Jewish areas in Rome and Venice.

Many European Jews suffered during the Crusades, when angry mobs attacked the first non-Christians that they found: the Jews. In 1347, a mysterious disease—the Black Death, or bubonic plague—spread across Europe, eventually killing half of Europe's population. Jews were accused of poisoning the wells that provided water. Many Jews were attacked and survivors fled eastward along the Danube Valley to Poland and Hungary, whose kings welcomed Jews to settle in their realms. Soon the area ruled by the Polish kings (at that time a large part of East Europe) would become home to Europe's largest Jewish population.

On March 31, 1492, King Ferdinand and Queen Isabella of Spain issued the Order of Expulsion that forced Jews to convert to Christianity or leave Spain.

In 1492 King Ferdinand and Queen Isabella united the Kingdom of Spain and declared the expulsion of all unconverted Jews under penalty of death. The Sephardic Jews fled to cities around the Mediterranean Sea, especially to those where they were welcomed by the Ottoman Empire, such as Istanbul and Salonika.

# A MODERN ERA

Life for Europe's Jews changed little until the French Revolution. France now defined its people as citizens, not as subjects of a king, and in 1791, the Republic of France granted full citizenship to the Jews of France. As Napoleon marched across Europe, so did the ideas of the French Revolution. Jews began to emerge from the ghettos and play a new role in the social and economic life of a new Europe. Some Jews, particularly in Western Europe, chose to assimilate, that is, blend into the larger communities of their countrymen. Farther East, Jews were still restricted by law in the Russian Empire to live in small towns, or shtetls, in an area designated the Pale of Settlement in the Ukraine and Poland.

The old empires of Europe were fading, and a new idea replaced them: the ideal of a national state. A national state was a land defined by the ethnicity of its people, not only by loyalty to a king or a religion. A wave of nationalist revolutions rocked Europe in 1848.

# THE NEW CENTURY

By the dawn of the twentieth century, Jewish life in Europe was at a crossroads. Zionism and socialism competed for

# ZIONISM

Two of Europe's peoples lacked the physical land needed to imagine a national state: the Jews and the Roma, or Gypsies. Around 1880 a Hungarian Jewish journalist named Theodore Herzl proposed a radical new idea: Shouldn't the Jewish people have a land of their own—the Zion promised to the Jewish people in the Bible? Various schemes were proposed. The British Empire was asked to look into colonizing Uganda with Europe's Jews. Argentina and Madagascar were also considered possible future Jewish states.

Many young Jews could not wait for the answer and began to walk to Palestine, a province of the Ottoman Empire, from small villages in Eastern Europe. By the time the movement for a Jewish homeland, now called Zionism, held a conference in Basel, Switzerland, in 1897, Ottoman Palestine was already home to thousands of pioneering Jews. The Basel conference decided to press for a Jewish settlement in Palestine. Across Europe Zionist youth groups formed, learning a new language—spoken Hebrew—and practicing farming and skills needed to homestead in the new land. Some were influenced by left-wing thought, such as Hashomer Hatzair, while some detested communism, such as Betar. All were well organized and in communication with other Zionist youth groups around Europe. When the Nazis arrived, young Zionists were often the first to organize effective resistance.

loyalty among educated Jews. Religious Jews felt resentment against those Jews who were no longer practicing their religion as a lifestyle. Many Jews used their new freedom to pack up and leave for greener pastures, immigrating to America or Canada, or joining the settlements in Palestine.

Disturbing signs were also growing in Europe. Anti-Jewish riots called pogroms were taking place in Russia, causing waves of Jews to flee to the west. The new arrivals were often less than welcome. In France, the trial for treason of a Jewish army captain, Alfred Dreyfus, divided the nation. In 1906, a book appeared claiming the world was controlled by a secret conspiracy of Jewish bankers. *The Protocols of the Elders of Zion* was, in truth, a forgery written by members of the Russian secret service, but it was widely translated and accepted as fact.

World War I began when a Serbian nationalist shot a member of the Habsburg royal family in Sarajevo, Bosnia, in

After World War I, many Germans felt that the Treaty of Versailles, signed in 1919, was unfair. Hitler focused this anger against the Jews.

1914. Within weeks Europe was involved in a terrible war with no real goal; it was war merely for the sake of war. World War I ended without any clear victory in 1918.

The Treaty of Versailles in 1919 forced Germany to accept harsh surrender terms that required it to disband its military and to pay a large sum of 132 billion marks for war reparations. (Germany made its final payment in 2010!) German soldiers, bitter about the German surrender, returned home to find the economy in ruins. People wanted to know who was to blame for their defeat. Many German newspapers claimed that Germany had been "stabbed in the back" by an inner enemy: the Jews, who were seen to be behind the recent communist revolution in Russia.

# HITLER: A PROPHET OF HATRED

In 1919, Adolf Hitler was an Austrian veteran of the German army living in Munich, Germany. In that year Hitler was hired by the German army to spy on a small, new anti-Semitic political party, the German Workers' Party. Hitler joined the party, however, which soon renamed itself the National Socialists, also known as the Nazi Party. Hitler had lived in Vienna and admired the anti-Semitic speeches of Vienna mayor Joseph Lueger, and he began to use hate language against the Jews in his speeches. Dr. S. D. Stein notes that as early as 1922, Hitler said, "If I am ever really in power, the destruction of the Jews will be my first and most important job."

Hitler was sent to jail for attempting to overthrow the German government in 1923. While in jail, Hitler wrote the book *Mein Kampf* (*My Struggle*), which stressed his hatred of Jews. Released from jail in 1924, Hitler was welcomed by cheering crowds ready to hear his message. Hitler understood the science of propaganda. His Nazi

In *The Last Days of Hitler,* historian Hugh Trevor-Roper called Adolf Hitler "among the 'terrible simplifiers' of history... the coarsest, cruelest, least magnanimous conqueror the world has ever known."

messages were designed to appeal to the largest amount of supporters, and this meant keeping his message simple: naming the enemies of the German people. Jews led the list, followed by communists, Roma (Gypsies), gay people, and Jehovah's Witnesses. The Nazis did well in elections, and when the seat of German government, the Reichstag building, was burned down on March 27, 1933, the Nazis blamed it on communists. An emergency decree was signed, allowing the Nazi party to take over the German government. A year later, Adolf Hitler was named Führer (Leader) of Germany.

# THE NAZI PATH TO HOLOCAUST

Nazi politics claimed that the German people were a superior Aryan race, which had rights over other, less racially pure people, such as Slavs and Jews. In the long term, the German people would need to expand German territory to include more agricultural land for Germans. This was called *lebensraum* or "living space." To do so, lesser peoples, called *untermentschen* ("lower people"), would have to be expelled from these lands, used as slave labor, or killed outright. The most fertile source for this new living space was to the east in Poland, Russia, and the Ukraine, home to the largest Jewish population in the world at the time.

## THE INVASION OF POLAND

To achieve lebensraum, Hitler began to rearm the German military, breaking the treaties signed at the end of World War I. The Germans first made claims to neighboring regions with German- speaking populations. In March 1938, Austria was united with Germany as one country, and in the fall of 1938, Germany annexed the Sudetenland of Czechoslovakia.

# BLOODLANDS

The Soviet Union was a dangerous threat to the German dreams of eastern expansion. Since 1921, Joseph Stalin had run the USSR as a virtual dictatorship. Stalin was a longtime communist revolutionary who had been born in Georgia, in the Caucasus Mountains. Under Stalin, Russia and the nations of the USSR had modernized at a rapid pace, but at the cost of millions of lives. During the early 1930s, Stalin was angered by the refusal of Ukrainians to join collective farms. Stalin cut off food supplies, causing a mass starvation that took more than three million lives. To this day, this is remembered in the Ukraine as the Holodmor, or "death by starvation."

By the time the Nazis and the Soviets signed a treaty to divide Poland in 1939, the border areas near Poland and Lithuania (today's Belarus) had already seen years of political mass murder, starvation, and deportations. During the first years of World War II, this region would become the area in which some of the most extensive murders against Jews and Poles would take place. It was to these eastern border regions that the Nazis transported Jews from all over Europe into ghettos. It was here that the Germans constructed the largest of their extermination camps. It was here, as well, that the most desperate of Jewish resistance fighters held out, knowing that there would be no mercy shown if they were ever caught.

Hitler grew bold with success and began to look east with hungry eyes.

Soviet leader Joseph Stalin hoped to prevent an alliance between Japan and Germany and wanted to be sure that Hitler agreed that the Soviet Union should have control over lands that lay along its western borders. On

The 1938 annexation of the German-populated Czechoslovak region of Sudetenland was the first step in rebuilding Hitler's idea of a new German Empire.

August 23, 1939, the German and Soviet foreign ministers signed a secret treaty promising nonaggression between the two powers: the Molotov-Ribbentrop Pact.

The German army then launched a surprise attack on Poland on September 1, 1939, using tanks, air attacks, and massive artillery fire to destroy the Polish army. The savage, quick attack tactic became known as blitzkrieg. Two weeks later, the Soviet army invaded eastern Poland. By October, Poland was defeated and divided. German troops roamed the streets rounding up Poles and Jews to be shot.

# GHETTOS IN POLAND

Only three weeks after the invasion of Poland, the Nazis issued a special law defining the treatment of Jews in Poland's German-occupied areas. As of September 21, 1939, Jews living in small towns and villages were to be moved into ghettos, special walled areas in larger cities.

The conditions in the ghettos were crowded and unhealthy. Food and medicine were scarce. Jews were only allowed outside the ghetto when they were taken to work on slave labor brigades. Often, a labor brigade would be marched out of the ghetto never to return. Their family members would be told they had been "transferred" to a work camp or labor battalion. In truth, many were taken into the forest to be shot or sent to death camps.

# THE DEATH CAMPS

Jews had no idea that the Germans were planning to separate them and, eventually, murder them. As the war progressed, ghettos under German control were emptied as the Jews who lived there were killed, starved, or transported to special concentration

camps to be murdered in a more industrial manner. By 1942, the Nazis had established six extermination camps in eastern Poland for the purpose of murdering Jews, Poles, Roma, and

Deported to ghettos, uncertain of their futures, Jews did whatever they could to survive.

Soviet war prisoners. These factories of death were located in Auschwitz (Oświęcim), Chełmno, Treblinka, Sobibór, Bełzec, and Majdanek. The Nazis knew that the camps needed to be kept secret. They rightly suspected that Jews and Poles would revolt if they knew the real function of the concentration camps.

In January 1942, leading Nazi officials held a conference in the Berlin suburb of Wannsee to develop a plan for a "Final Solution" for Europe's Jews: they would all be deported to Poland for extermination. But even before Wannsee, in December 1941, Hitler had met with the chief of the SS, a military police unit, to discuss what to do with the Jews in newly captured Poland and Russia. According to an interview for Yadvashem.org, Yehuda Bauer says that SS Chief Heinrich Himmler's notebook records Hitler's command to the SS: "Exterminate them on the pretext that they are partisans."

# SILENT RESISTANCE IN THE GHETTOS

Jews who found themselves crowded into the newly created ghettos had no idea of what their eventual fate would be. The Nazis did not announce their plans to exterminate the Jewish population of Europe, and many Jews expected to be rescued when England and France entered the war against Germany.

Behind the walls of the ghetto, Jews were cut off from communication with the outside world. Fear and confusion were widespread among the new arrivals. People with skills useful to the Nazis were given better treatment at first. Gertrude Boyarski of Derechin, Poland, remembered her family's arrival in a ghetto during an interview with the

Tough, resilient, and not bound by family ties, the first ghetto resistance fighters were often very young.

Jewish Partisans Educational Foundation (JPEF): "They told us all the rules and regulations. That we have to wear a yellow band. We have to walk in the gutter. We cannot walk at night. We have to work whenever they need us... So my father being a painter, they took him out of the ghetto. So they took us all out of the ghetto... And everybody called us 'The Living Jews.' My father said, 'No, we are not the Living Jews. We are Jews and we will be killed just the same.'"

To take up arms against an enemy as powerful as the German army would have seemed—to Jews forced from their homes into the new ghettos—to be an insane choice. But guns and bombs are not the only means of defiance. There were many other ways to resist. This simple refusal to lie down and starve to death was, in itself, the first act of resistance to the Nazis.

Resistance in the ghetto took many forms. When communication was forbidden, maintaining an illegal secret radio was a form of resistance. Secret newspapers were published and distributed. Spiritual resistance kept a sense of hope alive: religious ceremonies were performed in secret. Theater, music, and literary societies met quietly in basements. All of these were silent, invisible forms of resistance.

People who were allowed to move inside and out of the ghetto volunteered as couriers to carry letters and information. Some people smuggled food, usually with the help of Polish resisters outside the walls of the ghetto. Workers in slave labor factories often sabotaged German war efforts, repairing tanks and vehicles so that they would break down. Slave laborers in ammunition factories rigged weapons so that they would misfire or fail after a period of time.

Secret schools were set up for children in the ghetto. Charlene Schiff told the United States Holocaust Memorial Museum (USHMM) about her school in the Horochow ghetto: "In the very beginning, my mother and several other women organized a clandestine school for children who were below the age of work, and it was a wonderful thing because we had something to look forward to. It made us forget about the hunger... Several of the ladies, including my mother, would barter on the outside and they came home with crayons, with writing paper, with some books, and I

As had happened so many times in history, Jewish religious tradition often had to be practiced in secret.

mean they would tell stories, we would sing and we would color, and it was something to look forward to."

The Nazis appointed self-governing Jewish councils, called Judenrat, to keep order in the ghettos. People living in the new ghettos were faced with little choice. Cooperation could mean sacrificing family members during roundups or paying large bribes to save family from transports. In the huge ghetto in Łódź, the Judenrat council leader Khayim Rumkowsky became a hated figure among the Jews for giving into German demands, controlling food rations, and compiling lists for deportation. Rumkowsky believed he could save a majority of people if he sacrificed a portion. So he asked parents to give up their children to save the adults. A ghetto folk song written by Yankele Hershkowitz is remembered from the Łódź ghetto that says, "Our Khayim, Rumkowsky Khayim, performs miracles every day! He made a deal with the Angel of Death to provide more corpses every day! But Khayim just says 'Everything is fine!'"

When the Łódź ghetto was finally "liquidated" in 1944, Rumkowsky was sent with the other survivors to the concentration camp at Auschwitz. Within days, revenge-seeking Jewish inmates murdered him.

# LACHWA: THE FIRST GHETTO UPRISING

"Liquidation" was the term used by the Nazis when they wished to finally empty the Jewish population and ghetto. In some cases, the Germans actually did resettle a ghetto's inhabitants in a new, larger ghetto elsewhere. More often, liquidation meant shooting hundreds of people into mass graves in the forests. When the Jews of Lachwa (Łakhva) in occupied Poland heard news that massive pits had been dug at night outside the town, they had no illusions about their future.

When the Germans arrived with trucks to remove the Jews on September 2, 1942, the head of the Lachwa Jewish council, Dov Lopatin, set the Judenrat building on fire. Soon other ghetto buildings were burning, too. When Germans tried to load people onto trucks for deportation, Jews suddenly fought back with axes, knives, stolen grenades, and homemade bombs. Soon the Jews were returning fire with guns taken from fallen soldiers. More than one thousand Jews escaped into the forest and hid in the dense Pripyat swamps nearby, many eventually joining bands of partisan fighters.

The revolt in Łachwa was the first time a ghetto had risen up in arms against the Nazis. It would not be the last.

# CHAPTER 3

# RESISTANCE IN THE GHETTOS

Inside the ghettos, Zionist youth groups were secretly active, and groups such as the Jewish socialist Bund, which had organized labor unions before the war, were among the groups most involved in taking such daring steps to defy the Germans. It was often the younger people who were drawn to these early resistance groups. Sam Lato from the Baronovich (Baranowicze) ghetto told the JPEF, "Young people can do a lot of things; young people can do better than the older people because young people... they didn't have to defend their children. They didn't have to think about their wives or their brothers or their sisters... That's why most of... us partisans were young, 18, 19, 20, 25 was old already!"

## LET US NOT GO LIKE SHEEP TO THE SLAUGHTER!

The city of Vilna, known today as Vilnius, the capital of Lithuania, was for years a center of Jewish spiritual life. It was known as the "Jerusalem of Lithuania" and home to seventy thousand Jews, including many who had fled there as refugees from Poland. When Germany attacked the Soviet Union in June 1941, Lithuania was quickly taken and Vilna (Vilnius) had come under direct German control in August 1941.

During the summer, German and Lithuanian military units killed more than twenty thousand Jews, marching them out to the Ponary (Paneriai) Forest outside of the city and shooting them so that they fell right into open-pit graves. Jews remaining in the Vilna ghetto were set to work as slave labor, but during the fall thousands were taken out of the city and shot.

Before World War II, fifty-five thousand Jews lived in Vilna, making up 28 percent of the city's population. Today, only three thousand Jews remain in Lithuania.

# FACTORS AGAINST RESISTANCE

There were several reasons why Jews in the ghettos did not immediately fight against their oppressors. For one thing, they did not know what the immediate future held, and many hoped the war would soon end if England and France defeated Nazi Germany. The odds against an armed uprising were overwhelming. If the Polish army itself could not defeat the German army, what could a handful of unarmed Jews do?

The German tactic of "collective responsibility" also worked to keep resistance to a minimum. If a German soldier was found killed, an entire village might be murdered in revenge, as occurred in Lidice, Czechoslovakia, in 1942. Public hangings in the ghettos were a daily warning that resistance would mean the death of many innocent people as well.

At first, Jews in the ghettos had no weapons with which to defy the well-equipped Nazis. Guns were smuggled in when they could be found, but most were woefully inadequate compared to hefty German firepower. So valuable were guns that many partisan groups demanded that whoever wished to join them must provide their own gun. Aron Bell, the brother of forest partisan Tuvia Bielski, told the JPEF, "Arms? Without it you are nobody. This was your life, this was your freedom. A pistol, a rifle—this gave you everything. This gave you life."

In many regions, local Jews did not experience good relations with their non-Jewish neighbors. Many of the Jews living in the ghettos had only recently been resettled to these new areas from other countries, and often did not even speak the local languages. Making alliances with local non-Jews proved difficult for them.

When the Germans first arrived in Vilna, seventeen members of the Zionist youth group Hatzair Hashalom fled the city to hide in the countryside and were given shelter by a Polish Catholic nun, Mother Bertranda, in a convent just outside of Vilna. One of them, Abba Kovner, returned secretly to the ghetto to organize a meeting of young Zionists on New Year's Eve, 1941. Kovner was convinced that the Nazis planned to kill all the Jews of Europe without mercy and that the only choice was to fight. According to Michael Bart's book *Until Our Last Breath*, Kovner had written an announcement for the meeting, which said, "Hitler is scheming to annihilate all of European Jewry. The Jews of Lithuania were tasked to be first in line. Let us not go like sheep to the slaughter! It is true that we are weak and defenseless, but resistance is the only response to the enemy! Resist! To the last breath."

Vilna's United Partisan Organization (in Yiddish: Fareynikte Partizaner Organizatsiye or FPO) became the first secret organized resistance unit in a Jewish ghetto. They believed that their armed revolt would take place within the ghetto itself, so they immediately began smuggling guns into the ghetto. They placed their own members secretly among the Jewish ghetto police and guarded secret routes in and out of the ghetto to their hiding places in the forest and to Mother Bertranda's Catholic convent. The FPO built a secret headquarters and weapons factory in a basement beneath a library in the ghetto. They mapped all the alleys and cellars so that they could move through the ghetto undetected. They stockpiled guns and taught new members to make hand grenades from used electric lightbulbs. By the fall of 1942, the FPO had more than two hundred fighters. All they could do now was wait.

# ELSEWHERE IN EUROPE

As the Nazis began to occupy other countries in Europe, their policy toward the Jews remained the same: Jews were stripped of their human rights and ordered to wear yellow star badges on their clothing that identified them as Jews. They were ordered to appear for transportation to a collection camp and eventually deported to the east, usually to a ghetto in occupied Poland but later directly to one of the death camps.

The most common form of resistance available to Jews was simply to hide, usually with the help of brave non-Jewish friends. Anne Frank and her family hid in a tiny attic in Amsterdam, Holland, for two years before being arrested and sent to the Bergen-Belsen concentration camp in Poland in 1944, where she died of typhus fever two weeks before the liberation of the camp. Anne Frank's diary was found and published after the war.

Jews in France often worked with units of their local resistance called the maquisards. A group of young French Zionists formed the Armée Juive or Jewish Army, guiding groups of Jewish refugees to safety in neutral counties such as Switzerland or Spain. In Greece, Jews joined with non-Jewish partisan groups. As Leon Idas told the JPEF, "We are Jewish, and you know what happened to the Jews, I said… we didn't care if it was the Communists or Royalists or Democratic or Conservative, we come here to become partisan, to fight the common enemy."

When the Germans invaded Yugoslavia, roundups and massacres of Jews were so quickly carried out that the northern Yugoslav region of Voivodina became the first area of Europe to be declared Judenrein, or completely

In occupied countries, the Nazis forced Jews to sew yellow cloth stars on their clothing. This made them easily identifiable.

Marshall Josef Broz Tito's Yugoslav partisans forced the Germans to divert one-third of their army away from the Eastern Front. This helped guarantee Germany's defeat in World War II.

free of Jews. By 1941, most Yugoslav Jews had been murdered. That same year the Yugoslav communist leader Josef Broz Tito organized the war's most effective partisan movement. Tito directly ordered his partisans to assist Jews. More than four thousand Jews joined his partisan brigades, including many medical doctors. Tito's partisans were not separated by their ethnicity or religion, and Jews served alongside non-Jews. Tito's second in command, Moshe Pijade, was Jewish, as were partisan commanders Shmuel "Todorovich" Lerer and Rosa Papo, the first woman general of the Yugoslav army. The Yugoslav partisans forced the Germans to divert time, soldiers, and weapons from their war in Russia.

# CHAPTER 4
## THE GHETTOS EXPLODE

"Partisans are not greater heroes than other people," Miles Lerman told the JPEF. "They were just fortunate to be in a situation where they were able to get a hold of weapons, they were able to find a group of people that decided to resist. So instead of living on their knees, they decided to die on their feet. This is what a partisan is."

Warsaw, the capital city of Poland, was the site of the largest Jewish ghetto in Europe. In April 1940, an area of the downtown Warsaw was walled off to create a massive ghetto to house four hundred thousand Jews who had been deported from other cities and villages in Poland and Europe. Conditions in Warsaw were brutal. At first the Nazi strategy was to starve the Jews, issuing ration cards that limited Jews to only 180 calories of food a day, whereas a German received 2,500 calories worth of food. Abraham Levent told the USHMM that as a boy in the Warsaw ghetto, "I remember for a couple of weeks we just lived on sour pickles because on the street where we lived, there used to be a Polish factory that produced pickles. So I went with a friend of mine and somehow we got into that building at night and grabbed about six or eight cans, and we lived on that for a couple of weeks." By mid-1942, more than one

Facing a Nazi policy of starving the ghetto, Jewish and Polish partisans smuggled food to ensure adequate nutrition for children.

hundred thousand Warsaw Jews had died of starvation and disease.

On April 18, 1942, the Germans announced that Jews would be sent for "resettlement to the east." Throughout the summer of 1942, more than 250,000 people were herded onto freight trains in what the Germans labeled "The Great Action." Their destination, however, was not to eastern ghettos but to the death camp in Treblinka, where the Nazis murdered two hundred Jews at a time using carbon monoxide gas.

# POLISH AID TO JEWS

When the Germans invaded in 1939, members of the Polish government escaped to London, from which they re-formed into a Polish government in exile. One of their first efforts was to make contact with remaining units of the Polish army, which they organized as a partisan fighting force known as the Armia Krajowa, or Home Army. The Armia Krajowa was committed to fighting to regain Polish independence against both the German Nazis and the Communist Soviets who divided the nation between them after the invasions of 1939. In 1939 the Soviets had secretly executed more than twenty thousand captured Polish military and police officers in the Katyń forest in Russia. A victory by either the Germans or the Russians would mean a disaster for an independent Poland.

The Jewish partisans, however, often viewed the Soviets as the lesser of two evils, knowing that, as Jews, a German victory could only mean death. Many Zionist groups, such as Hashomer Hatzair, were making links to get supplies from Soviet partisans. Other Jewish groups, such as the Zionist Youth group Betar, distrusted the Soviets. The Polish Home Army, however, was notoriously full of anti-Semitic nationalists and was slow to arm Jewish partisans. Yet when the ghetto uprising broke out in April 1942, Polish Home Army units attacked Germans from outside the Warsaw ghetto, even attempting to blow up the ghetto walls.

In October 1942, the Polish Home Army, cooperating with Jewish groups, formed a secret organization called Żegota (Polish Council to Aid Jews). Żegota funneled food, money, and fake identification to Jews trapped in the ghetto. They set up a network of orphanages among Catholic convents and families to look after Jewish children smuggled out of the ghetto. Thousands of Polish Jews were saved by the actions of Żegota, which was recognized after the war by a memorial in Israel's Yad Vashem Holocaust Museum.

# THE WILL TO RESIST

By September 1942, only about fifty thousand Jews remained in the ghetto, and young survivors who belonged to Zionist youth groups Hashomer Hatzair and Dror prepared to fight back. They founded a resistance movement called the Jewish Combat Organization (in Polish: Żydowska Organizacia Bojowa, or ŻOB) and prepared by digging tunnels to connect underground cellars in the ghetto. Another Jewish fighting group, the ŻWW (Jewish Military Union) was led by Jews who had been Polish army officers. When the Germans attempted to finally clear the Jews out of the ghetto in January 1943, ŻOB and ŻWW responded by fighting back, armed with pistols and homemade bombs.

On April 19, 1943, the Germans entered the Warsaw ghetto on the first day of the Jewish holiday of Passover intending to liquidate the ghetto. David Jakubowski was with ZWW defenders who first attacked the Germans, and according to the archives of Yad Vashem, he said, "The Germans came into the Muranowska gate singing, happy. The Jewish boys knew that every bullet had to kill... And we had two flags on the building there—a Polish one and a Jewish one. When they stopped singing the Germans came under fire. And it was hell for them. They threw their guns and they ran away... now every piece of arms, every pistol, every gun, every submachine gun was collected. That's how the underground got submachine guns."

The German soldiers were shocked at the Jewish attack. The Germans had been trained to think of Jews as passive, unwilling to defend themselves. They now learned otherwise.

For more than a month, the desperate Jewish fighters in the Warsaw ghetto fought the Germans. From their

# MEMORY AS DEFIANCE: THE ONEG SHABBAT ARCHIVE

Memory can be a form of resistance as well. Very few people survived the Warsaw ghetto, but much of what we know about life and struggle there comes from a collection of documents that was buried in metal milk cans under the ruins of the ghetto. Emanuel Ringelblum was a historian who organized a group of writers, rabbis, and teachers into the Oneg Shabbat Society to document the daily realities of life in the ghetto. They collected more than twenty-five thousand diaries, letters, underground newspapers, legal decrees, and posters and programs from illegal concerts. These were placed in three large milk cans and some metal boxes and buried in the rubble of the ghetto during the spring of 1942. Dawid Graber, a nineteen-year-old student who helped bury the cans, slipped a note into one of them that read, "What we were unable to scream out to the world, we have concealed under the ground. One thing I am proud of, namely, that in these disastrous and horrible days I had been chosen to help bury the treasure, in order that you may know of the tortures and murders of the Nazi tyrants."

Two milk cans and boxes were found in 1946 and 1950. One is on display in Warsaw at the Jewish Museum, and the other is on loan to the United States Holocaust Memorial Museum in Washington, D.C. The third can has never been found.

underground bunkers the Jewish defenders crawled through a system of tunnels and over rooftops. They surprised the German troops with their stubborn will to survive and frustrated the Nazi command, which was anxious to destroy this threat to their idea of German

As the last Jews were rounded up, the Nazis set fire to the Warsaw ghetto. After the Second Warsaw Uprising in 1944, the Germans burned down the entire city.

superiority. Illegal shortwave radios carried the news of the Warsaw uprising to other ghettos. According to Yehiel E. Poupko, in April 1942 ZOB leader Mordechai Anielewicz wrote a letter: "The last wish of my life has been fulfilled. Jewish self-defense has become a fact... I am happy to have been one of the first Jewish fighters in the Ghetto. Where will rescue come from?"

The Germans showed no mercy, bombing and burning the ghetto to the ground in their search for Jewish holdouts. On April 29, the Germans took the ŻWW building on Muranowska Street. On May 18, 1942, the Germans attacked the headquarters of the ŻOB fighters at their basement bunker fortress at 18 Mila Street. With no hope for escape, the fighters, along with ŻOB leader Mordechai Anielewicz, chose to commit mass suicide rather than surrender. Scattered fighters continued resisting until May 16, when German Commander Jürgen Stroop blew up the Great Synagogue of Warsaw and the entire Warsaw ghetto was burned to the ground. Only a handful of fighters were able to escape through sewers and secret tunnels to be rescued by Polish Home Army fighters. One year later, in 1944, Jewish fighters joined the Polish Home Army in the final Warsaw uprising. The Nazis responded by bombing and burning 85 percent of Warsaw to the ground.

# VILNA REVOLTS

"Our fight was not for self preservation. It was not a question to save myself, to save you, to save a neighbor. It was to fight Germans," Abba Kovner recalled in an interview for the documentary film *Shoah*.

The news of the Warsaw ghetto uprising soon spread. During the summer of 1943, Jews in the Polish ghettos of Częstochowa, Białystok, Sosnowiec, and Będzin all attempted to revolt against the final German actions to transport them to the camps. All these revolts ended unsuccessfully.

In July 1943, the leader of the FPO resistance movement in Vilna, Yitzhak Wittenberg, was arrested. While he was being taken away, Wittenberg was freed in a daring rescue by FPO partisans. The Germans then declared they would destroy the entire ghetto if Wittenberg did not surrender. The next day Wittenberg gave himself up. Abba Kovner called for a general uprising, but angry ghetto crowds blamed the FPO for increasing the danger of Nazi retaliation and ignored Kovner's call for a revolt. Rather than risk betraying the names of his fellow partisans under torture, Wittenberg swallowed a poison capsule and died in his cell.

Abba Kovner became the leader of the FPO. On September 1, 1943, the Vilna ghetto was surrounded by Nazi troops with orders to round up five thousand Jews for transport to a slave labor camp in Estonia. Kovner ordered the FPO to begin the revolt, but before the weapons could be distributed, an entire FPO battalion was captured. Someone had betrayed the FPO to the Nazis.

Kovner again issued a call for the Jews of Vilna to join his fighters and resist the Nazis, who were now snatching Jews off the streets. When the ghetto did not erupt in support for Kovner's uprising, he quickly drew up another plan designed to prevent German patrols from finding the FPO's secret basement arms factory. German soldiers bombed the neighboring houses, but the Nazis gave up their attack without ever discovering the FPO hideout.

On the morning of September 23, 1943, Nazi SS Chief Bruno Kittel declared that the remaining Vilna ghetto residents were to pack their bags and prepare for deportation. The Vilna ghetto was being "liquidated." That evening, Abba Kovner and the remaining seventy FPO fighters escaped the ghetto by climbing through the sewer system. Unfortunately, the sewers did not lead them entirely outside of Vilna. For two days Kovner and his band hid where the Germans were least likely to look for them: in a basement below a German police station! From there they were able to make their way out to the Rudnicki Forest, where they contacted a small advance group of Soviet partisans.

The Soviets wanted the Jewish FPO units to join regular Soviet partisan groups, but Kovner knew that even among the communists anti-Semitism was widespread. Eventually, Kovner convinced the Russian commander to allow for independent Jewish partisan units under Soviet command. Kovner gave his partisan unit the name Nakam: the Hebrew word for revenge. They would become known as the Jewish Avengers.

# DEFIANCE IN THE DEATH CAMPS

The existence of the Nazi death camps at Auschwitz had been known since 1941, when Polish Home Army Officer Witold Pilecki volunteered to enter the camp as a prisoner. He sent reports on the conditions inside the camp to the Allies for three years before escaping. The Allies did not want to bomb the camp or its railway lines, however, because it was not considered an important military target. By the end of the war, at least three million Jewish people had been killed in the camps.

There were several kinds of concentration camps run by the Nazis: work camps, prisoner of war camps, slave labor camps, and resettlement camps. In extermination camps, most people were sent to their deaths on the day they arrived. The extermination camps were set up as killing factories and in most cases (Auschwitz being an exception) had living facilities only for those prisoners who worked as slave labor. The physical work of loading the bodies into the cremation furnaces and disposing of the remains was performed by crews of healthy younger prisoners called *Sonderkommando*. They were allowed to live for six months before they, too, were killed and replaced.

The Auschwitz camp was both a death camp and a forced labor camp. Younger inmates were more likely to revolt.

# TREBLINKA

Treblinka was the extermination camp to which most of the Jewish population from Warsaw was sent. In 1943, prisoners brought word of the Warsaw ghetto uprising and a group of Sonderkommando, led by Jewish prisoners who had been officers in the Polish Home Army, decided to attempt an escape. August 2, 1943, was a Monday, a day off for the German and Ukrainian guards at Treblinka,

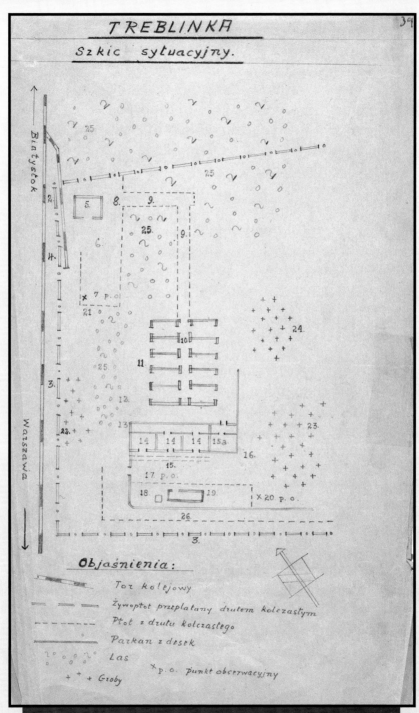

Most death camps lacked basic living facilities. No one was expected to survive long after arrival at Treblinka.

many of whom had gone to the nearby river to swim. Jewish Sonderkommando secretly stole guns and grenades from the warehouse and attacked the gates in the afternoon, setting the camp on fire. Hundreds of prisoners ran in all directions attempting to escape but were cut down by German guards on horseback. Only about 150 managed to escape into the woods, where many joined partisan units. The camp was never fully functional after the revolt, and it was shut down a year later after all evidence that it had ever been a death camp was carefully hidden.

# SOBIBOR

During the summer of 1943, the Sonderkommando prisoners working at the death camp in Sobibor noticed that fewer new prisoners were arriving. This meant that a camp would be closing and that the Sonderkommando themselves would soon be killed. One of the prisoners, Leon Feldhendler, began to draw up plans for an escape.

In August 1943, a new transport brought some Jewish prisoners of war from the Soviet army, led by Alexander Pechersky, who added valuable military skills to the group. According to the University of Southern California Shoah (USC Shoah) Archives, Regina Zielinsky recalled that the prisoners had no illusions: "We were told when we organized the escape, that if even one person should survive, the escape would be a success."

Those who rebelled at Sobibor were people facing certain death. They chose to take their chances and die on their feet.

On October 14, 1943, prisoners lured their guards into one of the barracks, killed eleven of the guards and the camp commander, and stole their guns. The escape was discovered, however, and six hundred prisoners rushed to get

47

# AUSCHWITZ: FACTORY OF DEATH

Auschwitz consisted of three camps. One was the main prison camp; one was Auschwitz-Buna, which was a forced labor camp for the German chemical company IG Farben; and finally, there was Auschwitz-Birkenau, the death camp. There was a separate camp for Roma prisoners, as well as a camp where Nazi doctors such as Josef Mengele performed horrific medical experiments on prisoners. Conditions were horrendous for all prisoners, as starvation and disease took their toll. Surrounded by barbed wire and guard towers, escape was nearly impossible. More than one million prisoners died at Auschwitz.

Prisoners arriving at Auschwitz were separated into groups as soon as they were unloaded from the arriving trains. Healthy young people who could work were "selected" and sent off to the labor camp, where the average life expectancy would be no more than three months. Leo Schneiderman, from Lodz, arrived in Auschwitz in 1944. He told the USHMM: "It was late at night that we arrived at Auschwitz... And everything went so fast: left, right, right, left. Men separated from women. Children torn from the arms of mothers. The elderly chased like cattle. The sick, the disabled were handled like packs of garbage... My mother ran over to me and grabbed me by the shoulders, and she told me 'Leibele, I'm not going to see you no more. Take care of your brother.'" Older people, women with children, and the sick were ordered to leave their belongings and marched into buildings to shower after their journey. They usually did not guess their fate until their last minutes. Instead of water, the shower faucets released deadly poison Zyklon B gas. The dead bodies were then cremated in furnaces by a special unit of Sonderkommando.

through the fences and gates to freedom. Tomasz Blatt, a survivor, described to USHMM, "I heard a shot, Sasha Pechersky jumped on the table, and he started to talk... 'The time did come that we will take revenge. We killed practically all the Germans. Now, let's stand up and fight our way out... If somebody of you will survive, you should remember to tell the world the story of Sobibor.'"

Almost half of the fleeing prisoners made it out to meet with partisan units in the woods. Esther Raab, a young woman prisoner, told USHMM that when she made it through the fence she saw the bodies of those who had been killed by land mines: "I noticed there are a lot of bodies already on the mines... I got a bullet shot from the tower right here, and I fell down. As I fell down, I was so much aware, and the will to live was so great, there's no measurements to it... and soon I reached the woods... I felt, I did it, I made it." SS Chief Heinrich Himmler ordered the closing and destruction of the Sobibor camp two days later.

# THE SONDERKOMMANDO REVOLT

Young Jewish members of the Auschwitz-Bireknau Sonderkommando had learned that the Nazi guards intended to kill them to hide any evidence of war crimes being committed at Auschwitz. Girls working as slave labor in the chemical factory smuggled small amounts of gunpowder to the Sonderkommando, from which they made bombs and grenades. On October 7, 1944, the Sonderkommando attacked their guards, throwing the SS commander into the oven itself, and blew up one of the crematoriums. About five hundred young Sonderkommando attempted to escape, fighting off the SS with shovels and sticks. Linda Breder was a young prisoner who witnessed

Ruins of the Auschwitz-Birkenau gas chamber and crematorium. The sign at Auschwitz's gate reads, *Arbeit Macht Frei* ("Work Will Set You Free"), a cruel lie to those who entered.

the revolt. She explained to the USC Shoah Archives, "There was fire and it was very, scary, we knew now it was the end for us. Late in the day they found all the

Sonderkommando, they shot them all… but from this time, there was no gassing. The Sonderkommando had blown up the gas chamber."

In November 1944, with Soviet troops approaching, SS General Himmler ordered the closing of Auschwitz and the destruction of all written records. Sixty thousand prisoners were forced on a death march to Bergen-Belsen concentration camp inside Germany itself, where the survivors were finally liberated by Soviet troops on January 27, 1945. Today, January 27 is celebrated worldwide as Holocaust Remembrance Day.

# CHAPTER 6

# INTO THE FORESTS

Outside the walls of the ghettos and the concentration camps, the deep forests of Eastern Europe offered the best hope for survival. German tanks and armored cars could not travel far in the roadless swamps, and German patrols rarely penetrated the deep, wet forests of Poland, the Ukraine, and Lithuania. When Abba Kovner and his surviving FPO fighters left Vilna, they headed to the nearby Rudnicki Forest, hoping to meet up with Soviet partisans.

Kovner found a small camp of Soviet parachutists who had linked up with local Lithuanian and Polish underground fighters. The Soviet partisans only accepted male fighters who provided their own guns. There were also Polish and Lithuanian partisans who doubted that the Jewish arrivals would be of any use to their cause. Abba Kovner decided that he would have to move his Jewish partisans to their own camp, where they would keep their weapons and allow the women to continue the partisan fight.

To survive in the woods, partisans cut down trees and dug deep into the ground to build underground log cabins called *zemlyankas*. The crowded zemlyankas served as camouflaged bomb shelters and kept the

# PARTISAN POETS

Poetry and song were important to ghetto survivors and partisans, providing distraction and culture during nights in the dark ghetto cellars and log zemlyankas. The theme of Jewish suffering is an old one in Yiddish literature. Yiddish language poets wrote poems and lyrics that were sung in the ghettos. These lyrics endure to this day. One song, written by Vilna poet Hirsch Gluck in May 1943, when he first heard about the uprising in the Warsaw ghetto, spread to become the anthem of the Jewish partisans. The song in Yiddish is called "Zog Nit Keynmol"

*Never say this is the final road for you,*
*Though dark skies may cover days of blue.*
*As the hour that we longed for is so near,*
*Our step beats out the message—we are here!*
*This song was written with blood and not with lead,*
*It is not a little tune that birds sing overhead.*
*This song a people sang amid collapsing walls,*
*With grenades in hand they heeded the call.*

Abraham Sutzkever came to be known as the poet of the partisans. Born in 1913 in Smorgon (Smorhon), Belorussia, he was deported to the Vilna ghetto in 1941. When the Nazis began looting books and works of art in the Vilna ghetto, Sutzkever worked to save and hide as many as possible. With his wife, he fled to the Narocz Forest to join the partisan band of Moshe Rudnitski, where he continued to compose poetry. "If I didn't write, I wouldn't live," Sutzkever told the *New York Times* in a 1985 interview. "When I was in the Vilna ghetto, I believed, as an observant Jew believes in the Messiah, that as long as I was writing, was able to be a poet, I would have a weapon against death."

*(continued on page 54)*

(continued from page 53)

*Did you ever see in fields of snow*
*Frozen Jews, in row upon row?*
*Breathless they lie, marbled and blue.*
*Of death in their bodies, no hint and no clue.*
*Somewhere their spirit is frozen and saved*
*Like a golden fish in a frozen wave.*
*Not speaking. Not silent. Just thinking bright.*
*The sun too lies frozen in snow at night.*

partisans warm and dry in winter. Food was always in short supply. Partisans ate a soup called balanda, made from boiled rye flour and swamp water. Local farmers were raided and "taxed" to provide food. Sam Lato described to the JPEF how armed partisans requested food from villagers: "When we went to a village, let's say, usually a village was like 50–60 kilometers [31–37 miles] away from us… We told them we are Jews, and we want a cow. And he went, he was scared of us, so he picked a cow and he gave it to us. Simple as that."

Kovner's FPO was a disciplined military unit that allowed only fit, young, armed fighters to join. Not far away, in the dense Naliboki Forest (in present-day Belarus) the Bielski brothers, led by Tuvia Bielski, who had served in the Polish army, were more welcoming. They fled the ghetto of Novogrodek (Navahrudak) in 1941 and began to offer shelter to any Jews who managed to find their hidden community of zemlyankas. They also sent scouts into the ghettos to bring people out. Soon there were more than 1,300 in the Bielski band, most of whom were women, children, and the elderly who would not find acceptance in other partisan units. Tuvia

Bielski's brother Aron recalled to the JPEF, "Tuvia was a real human being—if ten will survive, why wouldn't 20 survive? If it's not enough to go 20 miles [32 km] after food, so you go 30, you go 40. But it's better than to go to the slaughterhouse, is it not?" Allied with the Soviet partisans, the Bielski brothers set up entire workshops of Jewish craftsmen to repair weapons, sew uniforms, and make shoes for the many partisan bands hiding in the forest. Deep in the woods they built a hospital and schools. The Bielskis avoided violent confrontation with the enemy as much as possible to protect the

Jews in the Tuvia Bielski camp. The Bielski camp managed to save more than 1,500 refugee Jews hiding deep inside the dense forests.

many unarmed refugees among them, but Tuvia Bielski did assist Soviet partisan raids against the Nazis and their collaborators in the area. The link to Soviet partisans meant parachute drops of valuable arms and food for the forest partisans.

# THE ATTACK ON KONIUCHY

Most partisan actions consisted of small, subversive measures that helped cripple German military activity. Railroad supply lines were blown up using homemade bombs, German supply transports were destroyed, and collaborating units of local police were killed. Direct battle was avoided whenever possible—to lose a single life was a great loss. In January 1944, however, Kovner's Jewish Avengers, along with Soviet partisans, launched an attack on the village of Koniuchy (today Kaniūkai, Lithuania), where local collaborators had killed two captured partisan scouts and put their bodies on public display in the village. Kovner gave orders to the partisans that nothing was to be taken from Koniuchy—no food, no livestock, no valuables. The attack was to send a clear message of what would happen to any village that collaborated with the Nazis.

By the summer of 1944, the Germans were in retreat from the advancing Soviet army. The Soviets had slowly come to respect the Jewish partisans for their skills and stubborn resistance. As the Red Army retook the cities and towns along the Eastern Front, Jewish partisans were called to act as scouts, using their knowledge of the cities to lead the Russian troops against the German and local defenders. On July 14, 1944, the city of Vilna was in Soviet hands. Jewish partisans were allowed into the city they had fled years before, only to find the ghetto streets empty, their friends and families lost to the extermination camps. By the spring of 1945, many surviving Jews who returned home from concentration camps and partisan groups had come to the conclusion that there was no future for them in Europe. Many decided to follow the Zionist dream of settling in the land of Israel or leaving Europe for the United States, Canada, or Argentina. But Abba Kovner was not finished with the Germans yet. He wanted revenge.

# NAKAM: REVENGE

With the war's end, some Jewish partisans refused to give up the fight against the Nazis. Execution squads of Jewish survivors hunted former SS guards and concentration camp officers and shot them without interference from the Soviet army, while members of the British Palestinian Jewish brigade also conducted summary executions of Nazi officers. When the Germans surrendered in May 1945, Abba Kovner drew up his own plan to take revenge against the Nazis who had murdered six million Jews. He reformed his original partisan brigade known as Nakam (revenge) and now called it DIN (judgment.)

Kovner's plan was to murder six million Germans by poisoning the water supplies of major German cities. According to Dina Porat in her biography of Kovner, *The Fall of a Sparrow*, he wrote that he sought "an organized, unique vengeance... such as only those who have survived such a terrible murder are capable of doing. It is an idea any sensible person could see was mad... and perhaps worse than mad." Kovner smuggled cans of arsenic poison onto a British ship bound for Europe, but he was discovered and arrested by the British and sent to jail in

A U.S. soldier guards German POWs in Remagen, Germany. After the war, many Jewish partisans and ex-camp inmates vowed to take personal revenge against Nazis, even in prisoner-of-war camps.

Egypt. Members of DIN did, however, manage to use arsenic to poison the bread served to German prisoners of war (POWs) at an American POW camp near Nurnberg on April 14, 1946. Nearly four hundred German prisoners died.

Kovner was released from jail in Egypt and fought in Israel's 1948 war of independence. He eventually married his fellow partisan Vitka Kempner and became an award-winning poet and writer. He died in 1987. Tuvia Bielski eventually moved to the Bronx, New York, where he died in 1987. Abraham Sutzkever passed away in 2010 at the age of ninety-seven.

The generation that witnessed the Holocaust is aging rapidly and soon not one living person will personally remember the experience of the Holocaust. We

The Wall of Remembrance at the United States Holocaust Museum in Washington, D.C., preserves memories to educate future generations about the Holocaust.

must remember the Holocaust as the story of its victims, as well as the story of its heroes. Even tragedy has heroes.

Today, museums like the U.S. Holocaust Memorial Museum in Washington, D.C.; the Yad Vashem Holocaust Museum in Tel Aviv, Israel; and many more work tirelessly to document the memories of elderly people who lived through the Holocaust. It is the duty of the living to remember the lessons of the past, to give voice to the victims, and to be inspired by the bravery of those who chose to resist. The spirit of defiance in the face of evil will remain, throughout history, their greatest legacy.

# Timeline

**September 1, 1939** Germany invades Poland.

**September 28, 1939** The Soviet Union and Germany divide Poland between them.

**October 8, 1939** Nazis set up the first Jewish ghetto in Poland at Piotrkow Trybunalski.

**April 7, 1940** The concentration camp at Auschwitz in Poland is opened as a prison camp.

**December 31, 1941** In the Vilna ghetto, Abba Kovner calls for armed resistance to the Nazis.

**January 20, 1942** Nazi leaders in Wannsee, near Berlin, form a plan for the extermination of Europe's Jews called "the Final Solution."

**September 2–3, 1942** The Jews of the ghetto in Lachwa, in Belorussia, resist Nazi attempts to kill them; seven hundred are killed, and many flee to forests.

**January 1, 1943** Armed units of the Żydowska Organizacia Bojowa (Jewish Combat Organization, ŻOB) open fire on German army in Warsaw ghetto.

**April 19, 1943** The Warsaw ghetto revolt begins.

**August 2, 1943** Prisoner uprising in the Treblinka extermination camp.

**August 16, 1943** Inspired by news of the Warsaw uprising, Jews in the Bialystock ghetto resist being deported to the death camps. After almost a week, many escape to the forests, but forty thousand are sent to the death camps.

**September 1, 1943** Vilna resistance leaders call for armed struggle against the liquidation of the ghetto but are forced to escape to the woods due to lack of arms.

**October 14, 1943** Revolt of the prisoners at Sobibor death camp.

**December 22, 1943** In Kraków in southern Poland, Jewish partisans attack a group of German officers in a café, killing eleven.

**May 16, 1944** Roma prisoners at Auschwitz rise up and attack Nazi guards sent to destroy the Gypsy barracks.

**June 6, 1944** D-Day; the Allied forces invade Europe at Normandy beach.

**August 1, 1944** Second Warsaw Uprising. Polish Home Army rises against Germans; Germans respond by demolishing 85 percent of the Polish capital city.

**September 1, 1944** Slovak National Uprising; more than one thousand Jewish partisans take part in action to liberate Slovakia.

**October 6, 1944** Sonderkommando revolt at Auschwitz concentration camp, destroying crematorium IV.

**April 11, 1945** Prisoners at Buchenwald concentration camp near Berlin revolt and hold their guards prisoner until the arrival of Allied soldiers.

**May 7, 1945** Germany surrenders.

# Glossary

**ASSIMILATION** The process whereby a minority group gradually adapts to the customs and attitudes of the prevailing culture.

**COLLABORATOR** A person who cooperates with the enemy.

**CONCENTRATION CAMP** A camp where civilians, enemy aliens, political prisoners, and sometimes prisoners of war are detained and confined under harsh conditions. Since World War II, it has also come to include the Nazi extermination camps.

**DIASPORA** A geographically scattered population with a common origin from its original homeland.

**FORGERY** The process of making fake documents or trying to create a deceptive story presented as real.

**GENOCIDE** The deliberate destruction of an ethnic, racial, religious, or national group of people.

**GHETTO** A part of a city in which members of a minority group live, especially because of social, legal, or economic pressure.

**JUDENRAT** The Jewish councils appointed by the Nazis to run the daily life of the ghettos in World War II.

**LIQUIDATION** The term used by the Nazis to describe the final destruction and killing of Jews in the ghettos.

**NATIONALIST** A belief, creed, or political ideology that involves an individual identifying with, or becoming attached to, one's nation.

**PARTISAN** A member of an irregular military force formed to oppose control of an area by a foreign power.

**POGROM** A violent massacre or persecution of an ethnic or religious group, particularly one aimed at Jews.

**PROPAGANDA** A form of communication created to influence the attitude of the community toward some cause or position by presenting only one side of an argument.

**REPARATIONS** Payments intended to cover damage or injury inflicted during a war.

**ZIONIST** A form of nationalism of Jews and Jewish culture that supports a Jewish nation-state in Israel.

# For More Information

Anti-Defamation League (ADL)
605 Third Avenue
New York, NY 10158
(212) 885-7700
Web site: http://www.adl.org
The Anti-Defamation League was founded in 1913 to stop
the defamation of the Jewish people and to secure jus-
tice and fair treatment for all. Its Web site contains
educational materials on the Holocaust.

Holocaust and Human Rights Education Center
Four West Red Oak Lane, Suite 330
White Plains, NY 10604
(914) 696-0738
Web site: http://www.holocausteducationctr.org
The Holocaust and Human Rights Education Center was
founded in 1990 to memorialize the victims of the
Holocaust and to honor the survivors, rescuers, and
liberators.

Jewish Partisan Educational Foundation (JPEF)
2107 Van Ness Avenue, Suite 302
San Francisco, CA 94109
(415) 563-2244
Web site: http://www.jewishpartisans.org
The mission of the JPEF is to develop and distribute effective educational materials about the Jewish partisans and
their life lessons, bringing the celebration of heroic

resistance against tyranny into educational and cultural organizations.

Organization of Partisans Underground Fighters and
    Ghetto Rebels in Israel
Arlozorov Street 102
P.O. Box 16146
Tel Aviv
Israel
(972-3)5273564
Web site: http://eng.thepartisan.org
Dedicated to preserving the heritage of Holocaust resistance,
    the Organization of Partisans Underground Fighters and
    Ghetto Rebels in Israel is completely based on volunteers.
    It represents the underground fighters, their problems, and
    their needs.

Sarah and Chaim Neuberger Holocaust Education Centre
4600 Bathurst Street, 4th Floor
Toronto, ON M2R 3V2
Canada
(416) 631-5689
Web site: http://holocaustcentre.com
Through its museum and programs, the Sarah and Chaim
    Neuberger Holocaust Education Centre generates knowl-
    edge and understanding about the Holocaust and serves as
    a forum for dialogue about civil society for present and
    future generations.

U.S. Holocaust Memorial Museum
100 Raoul Wallenberg Place SW
Washington, DC 20024-2126
(202) 488-0400
Web site: http://www.ushmm.org
A museum, research center, and memorial to the Holocaust,
the U.S. Holocaust Memorial Museum inspires citizens and
leaders worldwide to confront hatred, prevent genocide,
and promote human dignity. Its Web site features extensive
online resources, videos, and more.

USC Shoah Foundation
Institute for Visual History and Education
650 West 35th Street, Suite 114
Los Angeles, CA 90089-2571
(213) 740-6001
Web site: http://sfi.usc.edu
Inspired by his experience making *Schindler's List*, Steven
Spielberg established the Survivors of the Shoah Visual
History Foundation in 1994 to gather video testimonies
from survivors and other witnesses of the Holocaust. In
2006, the foundation became part of the University of
Southern California in Los Angeles, where the testimonies
in the Visual History Archive will be preserved in perpetuity.

Vancouver Holocaust Education Centre
50 - 950 W 41st Avenue
Vancouver, BC V5Z 2N7
Canada

(604) 264-0499
Web site: http://www.vhec.org
The Vancouver Holocaust Education Centre was
    founded in 1983 by survivors of the Holocaust. It is a
    teaching museum and a leader in Holocaust educa-
    tion in British Columbia, reaching more than fifteen
    thousand students annually.

Yad Vashem: The Holocaust Martyrs' and Heroes'
    Remembrance Authority
P.O. Box 3477
Jerusalem
Israel 9103401
(972-2) 644-3712
Web site: http://www.yadvashem.org
Established in Israel in 1953 as the world center for docu-
    mentation, research, education, and commemoration
    of the Holocaust, Yad Vashem safeguards the memory of
    the past and imparts its meaning to future generations.

# WEB SITES

Due to the changing nature of Internet links, Rosen
Publishing has developed an online list of Web sites related
to the subject of this book. This site is updated regularly.
Please use this link to access the list:

http://www.rosenlinks.com/DHH/Resist

# For Further Reading

Altman, Linda Jacobs. *The Warsaw Ghetto Uprising: Striking a Blow Against the Nazis.* Berkeley Heights, NJ: Enslow Publishers, 2011.

Arens, Moshe. *Flags Over the Warsaw Ghetto: The Untold Story of the Warsaw Ghetto Uprising.* Springfield, NJ: Gefen Books, 2011.

Bart, Michael. *Until Our Last Breath: A Holocaust Story of Love and Partisan Resistance.* New York, NY: St. Martin's Press, 2008.

Bauer, Yehuda. *A History of the Holocaust.* Danbury, CT: Franklin Watts, 2002.

Bergen, Doris, L. *War and Genocide: A Concise History of the Holocaust.* Lanham, MD: Rowman and Littlefield Publishers, 2009.

Bialowitz, Phillip. *A Promise at Sobibor: A Jewish Boy's Story of Revolt and Survival in Nazi-Occupied Poland.* Madison, WI: University of Wisconsin Press. 2008.

Brzezinski, Matthew. *Isaac's Army: A Story of Courage and Survival in Nazi-Occupied Poland.* New York, NY: Random House, 2012.

Cohen, Rick. *The Avengers: A Jewish War Story.* New York, NY: Random House, 2001.

Cymlich, Israel. *Escaping Hell in Treblinka.* New York, NY: Yad Vashem and the Holocaust Survivors Memoirs Project, 2007.

Duffy, Peter *The Bielski Brothers: The True Story of Three Men Who Defied the Nazis, Built a Village in the Forest, and Saved 1,200 Jews.* New York, NY: Harper Collins, 2003.

Frank, Anne. *Tales from the Secret Annexe.* London, England: Halban Publishers Limited, 2010.

Freiberg, Dov. *To Survive Sobibor.* Springfield, NJ: Gefen Books, 2007.

Levine, Allen. *Fugitives of the Forest: The Heroic Story of Jewish Resistance and Survival During the Second World War.* Guilford, CT: Globe Pequot Press, 2010.

Margolis, Rachel. *A Partisan from Vilna.* Brighton, MA: Academic Studies Press, 2010.

Porat, Dina. *The Fall of a Sparrow: The Life and Times of Abba Kovner.* Stanford, CA: Stanford University Press, 2009.

Rappaport, Doreen. *Beyond Courage: The Untold Story of Jewish Resistance During the Holocaust.* Somerville, MA: Candlewick Press, 2012.

Seiden, Othniel J. *The Remnant: The Jewish Resistance in WWII.* Parker, CO: Thornton Publishing, 2008.

Shor, Essie. *Essie: The True Story of a Teenage Fighter in the Bielski Partisans.* Bryn Mawr, PA: Mindfulness Publishing, 2009.

Snyder, Timothy. *Bloodlands: Europe Between Hitler and Stalin.* New York, NY: Basic Books, 2010.

Tec, Nechama. *Defiance.* New York, NY: Oxford University Press, 1993.

Yoran, Shalom. *The Defiant.* Garden City, NY: Square One Publishers, 2003.

Zissman, Harold. *The Warriors: My Life as a Jewish Soviet Partisan.* Syracuse, NY: Syracuse University Press, 2005.

# Bibliography

Anti-Defamation League. "Yehuda Bauer, Historian of the Holocaust." Retrieved August 29, 2013 (http://archive.adl.org/education/dimensions_18_1/portrait.asp).

Arad, Yitzhak. "The 'Final Solution' in Lithuania in the Light of German Documentation." YadVashem.org. Retrieved September 4, 2013 ( http://www.yadvashem.org/untoldstories/documents/studies/The_Final_Solution.pdf).

Bart, Michael. *Until Our Last Breath: A Holocaust Story of Love and Partisan Resistance.* New York, NY: St. Martin's Press, 2008.

Bauer, Yehuda. *A History of the Holocaust.* Danbury, CT: Franklin Watts, 2002.

Bauer, Yehuda. "Interview with Prof. Yehuda Bauer. Director of the International Center for Holocaust Studies of Yad Vashem." January 18, 1998. Retrieved September 2, 2013 (http://www.yadvashem.org/odot_pdf/Microsoft%20Word%20-%203856.pdf).

Brave Old World. *Dus Gezang fin Geto Lodzh–Song of the Lodz Ghetto.* Music CD. Munich, Germany: Winter and Winter, 2005.

Dawidowicz, Lucy S. *The War Against the Jews, 1933–1945.* New York, NY: Holt, Rinehart and Winston, 1986.

Facing History. "The Warsaw Ghetto Uprisings." Retrieved August 22, 2013 (http://www.facinghistory.org/sites/facinghistory.org/files/jews_of_poland_ch6_0.pdf).

Israeli Foreign Ministry, and Joseph Telushkin. *Jewish Literacy*. New York, NY: William Morrow and Co., 1991.

Jewish Virtual Library. "Archaeology in Israel: Masada Desert Fortress." Retrieved October 25, 2013 (http://www.jewishvirtuallibrary.org/jsource/Archaeology/Masada1.html).

Kovner, Abba. "Transcript of the Shoah Interview with Abba Kovner." Retrieved September 12, 2013 (http://resources.ushmm.org/intermedia/film_video/spielberg_archive/transcript/RG60_5017/A2E8DDA1-80C8-4C01-AB31-2C8C2BFB89D8.pdf).

Kovner, Vitka. "A Partisan's Resolve." Retrieved September 13, 2013 (http://www.yadvashem.org/yv/en/pressroom/magazine/pdf/yv_magazine22_p4.pdf).

Morcheles, Barbara Wind. "The Myth of Jewish Non-Resistance During the Holocaust – Abraham Sutzkever: A Model of Resistance, Revenge and the Discourse of Consolation." 2000. Retrieved September 4, 2013 (http://scholarship.shu.edu/cgi/viewcontent.cgi?article=1036&context=theses).

Paul, Mark. *Wartime Rescue of Jews by the Polish Catholic Clergy*. Toronto, ON, Canada: Polish Educational Foundation in North America, 2009. Retrieved September 10, 2013 (http://www.savingjews.org/docs/clergy_rescue.pdf).

Porat, Dina. *The Fall of a Sparrow: The Life and Times of Abba Kovner.* Stanford, CA: Stanford University Press, 2009.

Poupko, Yehiel E. "The End of Jewish Warsaw." 2013. Retrieved October 31, 2013 (http://www.juf.org/news/world.aspx?id=415910).

Ringelblum, Emmanuel. "Diary of the Warsaw Ghetto." 1942. (http://jewishcurrents.org/wp-content/uploads/2010/02/Emanuel-Ringelblums-Diary-translated-by-Max-Rosenfeld1.pdf ).

Romano, Jasa. "Jews of Yugoslavia, 1941–1945. Victims of Genocide and Freedom Fighters." Belgrade, Yugoslavia, 1980. Federation of Jewish Communities of Yugoslavia. Retrieved September 5, 2013 (http://www.jasenovac.org/images/jews_of_yugoslavia_1941_1945.pdf).

Snyder, Timothy. *Bloodlands: Europe Between Hitler and Stalin.* New York, NY: Basic Books, 2010.

Stein, S. D. "Statements by Hitler and Senior Nazis Concerning Jews and Judaism." Retrieved October 31, 2013 (http://www.ess.uwe.ac.uk/genocide/statements.htm).

Yad Vashem Exhibitions. "To Live with Honor and to Die with Honor." Retrieved September 2, 2013 (http://www.yadvashem.org/yv/en/exhibitions/live_with_honor/religious_observance.asp).

Yad Vashem Exhibitions. "Voices from the Inferno: Holocaust Survivors Describe the Last Months in the

Warsaw Ghetto." Retrieved August 22, 2013 (http://
www.yadvashem.org/yv/en/exhibitions/warsaw
_ghetto_testimonies/index.asp).

Yad Vashem Shoah Resource Center. "Lithuania."
Retrieved September 21, 2013 (http://www
.yadvashem.org/odot_pdf/Microsoft%20Word%20
-%206436.pdf).

Yad Vashem Shoah Resource Center. "The 'Final
Solution'—A Bureaucratic Process or an Ideological
Genocide?" January 18, 1998. Retrieved October 31,
2013 (http://www.yadvashem.org/odot_pdf/
Microsoft%20Word%20-%203875.pdf).

Yoran, Shalom. *The Defiant.* Garden City, NY: Square
One Publishers, 2003.

# Index

# ABOUT THE AUTHOR

Robert Z. Cohen was born in New York City. Cohen studied cultural anthropology at Boston University in Boston, Massachusetts. He is the son of a Holocaust survivor, and he moved to Budapest, Hungary, in the 1990s to research and record Romani and Jewish folk music traditions across Eastern Europe. He met dozens of elderly Jewish resistance fighters and survivors in the course of his research and heard firsthand stories of their experiences. He works as a journalist, travel guide writer, and musician. Cohen plays the violin and leads his own klezmer band playing Jewish folk music on tours around Europe and North America.

# PHOTO CREDITS